NOT MARKED ON THE MAP

Hanns Cibulka

Translated by EWALD OSERS

AQUILA *POETRY*

BRITISH LIBRARY CIP DATA

Cibulka, Hans
Not marked on the map : selected poems.
I. Title II. Osers, Ewald
831'.914 PT2663.12

ISBN 0-7275-0317-0
ISBN 0-7275-0318-9 Pbk
ISBN 0-7275-0319-7 limited ed. cased

Of this first edition, 25 copies have been signed and numbered by the author and translator.

AQUILA PUBLISHING COMPANY
an imprint of
Johnston Green Publishing (UK) Ltd
PO Box 1, Portree, Isle of Skye, Scotland IV51 9BT

INTRODUCTION

The unfortunate division of Europe, and more particularly of Germany, has somehow conditioned us to thinking of "East Germany" as of some far-away region, somewhere near the Balkans or on the fringe of the Russian steppe. How easy it is to be brainwashed by words.

The fact is that the traditional German term for Germany east of the Elbe, the territory of the German Democratic Republic, is *Mitteldeutschland,* central Germany, and thàt, far from being a border province, it has for centuries been the heartland of German culture. The Wartburg, in Thuringia, was a favourite Court of the *minnesingers,* the Middle High German minstrel poets of the 12th and 13th centuries, and a few hundred years later it was the place where Martin Luther began his translation of the New Testament into German. Weimar in the late 18th and early 19th century was perhaps the most enlightened German princely Court, the place where Goethe lived and worked. Jena is associated with Friedrich Schiller, Fichte, Hegel and many other outstanding representatives of German culture; Gotha was an important landmark in the history of German socialism. Johann Sebastian Bach wrote his immortal music mainly for the church of St. Thomas in Leipzig. Meissen was the place where the Elector of Saxony (who was also King of Poland), residing in Dresden, established Europe's first – and probably most famous – porcelain manufactory. And Leipzig in the second half of the 19th century became the centre of German book publishing. A region, therefore, right in the mainstream of German cultural and literary tradition.

All this is not to deny the existence of another literary trend, the "Sarmatian" poets: their eyes turned eastward to the border – hostile until not so long ago – between the Germanic and the Slav (or Balto-Slav) worlds, between European urban or settled-rural civilisation on the one side and a mysterious world of vast steppes on the other, with ancestral memories of fierce horsemen out of the East. It may well be that the Meads' excellent translations of Johannes Bobrowski and Michael Hamburger's equally excellent translations of Peter Huchel have led the English reader to assume that that was the character of all GDR poetry.

Hanns Cibulka's roots, however, both biographically and artistically, are Central European. He was born in Jägerndorf (Krnov) in the then German-speaking northern border region of Czechoslovakia, in 1920. Following the region's occupation and incorporation in Hitler's German Reich, Cibulka was called up for the German Army, served in Italy and Sicily, was taken prisoner by the British, and did not return from captivity until 1948. He settled in the GDR — German nationals from the border regions were expelled from post-war Czechoslovakia — studied librarianship in Berlin, and since 1952 has been Director of the Heinrich Heine City and District Library in Gotha.

These outward biographical signposts provide — as he himself points out — some important clues to his poetic experience and development. He declares his indebtedness to three poets: "Rilke, on account of my origin; Hölderlin, essentially because of my war years in Sicily and Italy; Ungaretti, a poet who has accompanied me to this day". If it is not presumptious for a translator to go beyond an author's self-analysis, I would say that Cibulka's roots (like Rilke's) in the overlapping and intermingling German-Czech cultural sphere, are reflected not only in his poetry *(Kuks, Polish Icons)* but also in his prose writings and in the fact that he has translated Czech poetry. I also have the impression that Sicily and Italy — in addition to and beyond Hölderlin — provided a more direct experience of classical antiquity, one which is reflected in many of Cibulka's poems. Another very important strand of his work is his deep involvement in music — and this emerges not merely from the poems on specifically musical subjects.

Cibulka is a poet of allusion and evocation: "naturalistic description destroys man's imagination", he says in an essay, "and makes the reader — as Goethe once put it — participate in 'faithfulness to nature' rather than in 'artistic truth'. The poetic image on the other hand, springs from the real sphere of our world: it grows out of it, but must not lose itself in objects or events. Showiness, provocativeness, surprise effects are not enough. The image must be like a flash of lightning, opening new horizons to the reader and revealing the spiritual background of life."

Hanns Cibulka is a newcomer to the English reader of poetry. I hope he will be a familiar name before long.

E.O.

CAPE ARKONA

Once
it was the eagle,
the falcon rampant,
heraldic symbols
on armour
and shield.

Today
it is the white
wild birds,
winging their way
up the coast,
sunlight
in their plumage.

The whole sky rings
with their trumpeted
"Ank-ho".

Swans, swans,
with their flight
winding white ribbons
round the earth,
when did we ever
catch such a
picture?

MUSICA ANTIQUA BOHEMICA

FRANZ BENDA : UN POCO ANDANTE

For Elisabeth and Reiner Kunze

A flute song
stolen from the wind's lips,
I advance slowly,
a man
who knows his way
no longer needs to hurry.

In the hop garden
I encounter the dusk,
in the grasses I see
its step,
already a shadow lies
across the track.

The light is fading,
the constellation homeland
is shining

wordlessly.

KUKS

Your glories,
Matthias Bernard Braun,
have stepped down
from their plinth,
no one knows
where
they have gone.

The angel
of annunciation
has departed,
he too
failed to leave
an address.

The days
flake off,
lime
on the tree trunks,
the terrace
in front of the church
is deserted.

Left behind
are a few inscriptions
chiselled
into the sandstone
plinth.

POLISH ICONS

I

The angel
in the bend of the Vistula
has scorched
wings.

Faint
distant lightning
in the apse.

Man,
the flaming cloth
of cities
as a standard,
is on the march
to reconnoitre
Hell.

II

The peasants
kneel in the honey light
of candles.

The priest
in his chalice carries
the body of the Lord.
the blood
we have shed.

The slain
enter
in a cloak
of purple.

HYPERION 1943

I

I came to meet you
at the wall of Syracuse,
fleeing fatherland.

Segesta
I saw
from the jeep,
parachute silk
dotted the fields.

Smoke shells
streaked up
into the antique blue.

In the villages
night landed,
tracer at its neck.

II

Land of arid limestone,
poetry has emigrated,
on crutches
the words parade
past the Forum Romanum.

With flag cloth
they cover their nakedness,
denying the wind
the message
it brings from other lands,
each open word
a trapdoor.

O my Bellarmin,
I would like to promise you
a better letter
from the land of oranges,
but my house
has fallen silent,
the windows
have learned to see.

MALARIA

At midnight
the doctor steps up to the bed,
hygienically white,
fever chart
in hand.

Violent shivers,
the teeth
chattering against the edge
of the cup,
the skin yellow
with atebrin.

I grope
along the fever's wall:
tulip fields
blooming
on snowy slopes
of Mount Etna,
in the lava flow Empedocles,
a bullet lodged
between his ribs.

In the Strait
o Messina
I cast
the last oar
into the sea.

Boat,
smashed
in the wind's laughter,
two garments
I leave to
earth.

LUDWIG VAN BEETHOVEN
STRING QUARTET IN C SHARP MINOR OP. 131

No
tubas or trumpets,
two violins
walking in front of me,
a cello
and a viola.

"Awakening
of joyful feelings
on arrival in the country,
scene by the brook",
how far back it all lies,
this audible landscape.

I
set my counterpoint
far
    out
        into
            space.

LIBUSSA

In memoriam
Vítězslav Nezval

Built upon
the hills of Resurrection,
Praga Regia,
at your feet
the speaking waters,
a cross of roses
under the threshold
of ice.

In the name of the Lord
I pin my prophecies
to the mantle of kings,
I show you
the head of John
under the guillotine,
the bullet-hole
in the Bohemian
monstrance.

I name you
the name of the saints,
their feet
broken
in the "Spanish boot",
Huss,
a torch
in the shadow
of the Castle.

Holy Nepomuk,
take your pencil
between your teeth,
even the Golem
will crumble
to ask again,
truth
doesn't need much
paper.

NOTE: According to traditional Czech legend Libussa founded the Přemyslid dynasty. She is venerated as a priestess and prophetess.

I GAVE YOU NAMES

Since my childhood
you have pursued me,
entering and leaving
through my words,
sitting, day after day,
at my table.

Behind my sense
you flash
more brightly
than the bundled light
of a laser.

Since my childhood
I've asked myself who you are
who walk in front of my life,
warning me
whenever the roads become
unsafe.

I gave you names
but you
invariably said
No!

And when breath
no longer clouds the mirror,
time
poured like water into water,
tell me, will you still
insist on your
silence?

KREMENEZ

Land,
I have half-forgotten
your language,
my grammar
has gone barbaric,
but year after year,
when the December wind comes,
I return to Kremenez,
to the village
with the different sky.

There my thoughts do not
tap at the window
like a homeless bird,
there you spread for me
a table with your words,
there the grain,
even in the ringing frost,
still silently grows
under the blanket
of sleep.

ALL SOULS

In my homeland, in November,
on All Souls Day,
my mother placed
a burning candle on the table,
let us remember the dead, she would say,
the world is full of their light,
which we don't see.

How they came,
the ones I lived with,
hurtling down
the slopes of Monte Cassino,
all killed in action
in sand-coloured uniforms.

And with horror
I watched
the dust rising
from the graves,
goose-stepping
through the
streets.

Soldiers,
lay down
your rifles,
what counts today is
courage in the face of
your conscience.

SKY FULL OF SWALLOWS

It's easy
to live on
the sun's shores,
my delicate
wind-swift bird.

The bright
open landscape
with olive leaf,
that is your home,
high above the blue
bed of rivers.

What are they to you,
the proud flight
of the eagle,
the lightning
in the eyes
of the owl?

In the elm's light
of night
you return to the
village,
domestic
is what you are
called.

My smoke-blue
queen,
with you would I live
by a river
which never
darkens.

GEODESY

Between surveyor's pole,
angle mirror and prism
the age-old picture,
a bridge
over the stream.

Straight lines
are pegged out,
fields
by invisible lines
bisected into
triangles.

Schloss Tenneberg
with its dark forests
held balanced
in the landscape,
levelled.

Not measurable
the trees' shadows,
the children's games,
untraceable
in the landscape
memory
stands still.

PO CHÜ-I

The news
from Ch'angan is gloomy,
the imperial guard
has occupied the city gate,
artificial birds
sing in the branches.

I live
near Loyang,
a captive of the mountains,
my hut is small,
no bigger than
an awl's point.

My courtier's robe
with hibiscus flowers
is pawned,
my orders are cast away.

With different eyes
I view the landscape,
left blank all deception,
a few strokes
are sufficient
for its profile.

Wherever
the tree may stand
the wind
will find it.

OSIP MANDELSHTAM

They nailed your tongue
which uttered
the idea's lightning
to the doorpost,
a warning
to others.

Metal fists
reached for the stars
but you
endured
deportations.

Yet your word,
fireproof,
ultimate homeland,
resisting
any weapon.

SONATA IN C

DEDICATION

Through the hair-shirt
of my age
I'm hit by the picture
of your verse.

Giuseppe Ungaretti,
under your umbrella pines
I want to walk homewards
when the cicada,
evening-bright,
turns the earth into
a song.

ALLEGRO

Thatched roofs,
on the path's edge
Our Lady
in wood
black
from the peasants'
prayer.

Hop-poles,
maize
with dry leaves,
the river
ties a blue ribbon
round the forest's
knee.

Every stone
was light,
even the thought
without shadow.

At nightfall
the harsh signals
from the barracks.
The mountain
a wall
of sleep.

The stars,
flowering boughs
above the earth.

Father,
let us sleep
in the field of lilies.

ANDANTE CON VARIAZIONI

November,
the weeping willows
stand unkempt.
Their feet in
fog boots.

The land
is without soul,
the helmet hides
the rose.

Silver trumpets
blind from
hoar-frost.

VAR. I

In my homeland
the fountains are frozen,
jug of childhood,
who has removed you
so far into the mountains?

Torn
from the lips
is the talk.

Each morning
to expunge
one's own name
from the day's tablet,
posters
over one's heart.

Crouching at night
in the hot cinders:
the voices of
the dead.

The masts
are struck,
the stork's nest
on our roof
stands empty.

VAR. II

The word
no longer reaches
the stone
of Golgotha.

Flame throwers.

Each day
has the shape of
a coffin.

The letters
we write
blue
with frost.

VAR III

No shroud.
The names
of the murdered
burned into
the bitter grey
of the wailing wall.

At your feet
the dust is
radiant.

MOLTO ADAGIO

In many lands' shadow
have we slept,
on the pyre
of the years,
now I arise
to look for the word
we all understand.

I with my nostalgia
for Germany,
that land of tomorrow,
where I no longer envy the bird
its wings.

Snowfall.

Soldiers
once more bivouacking
on the field of glory,
Christ
is wearing a crown
of strontium
on His head.

And I
have nothing
but the word,
this landscape
with the sevenfold
echo.

ALLEGRO CON SPIRITO

You've wintered
in the bunker,
survived
the nights as
a partisan.

Life,
I once more want
to write your name,
your lasting truth,
I hear it
in the dove's mating call,
in the seed grain
conversing with the earth,
a hand's breadth
below the day.

The passion
has died away,
the birds
are building
a nest
in their song.

SIRENS

I need
no wax for my ears,
no mast
to be lashed to.

On their silvery song
I sharpen
my thoughts.

GALE

A gale
blows round my house,
at night it rattles the beams
and flings a lump of clay
at my door.

In the
metal tops
of the pines
it hoists the flag,
then stops
and lays the fragments
of my childhood,
the humble village
with Moravian peasants,
outside my window.

Its silence is
a dash, a pause,
then it slams its fist
into the
forest's neck.

Squalls like sailcloth
crack against the wall,
oh this hunger
for distance,
for space.

Gale,
the air
in my room
is spent,
I fling
the window open.

"Where shall I start?"
I yell
into its face.

"There,
where your questions
are open!"

AERIAL

In the hours of darkness
the voices of the world
chase over my roof
into my room.

I hear
hard metal
in the words of the politicians.
Antigone shouts:
Why shouldn't I bury
my brother?
Behind the jazz curtain
I listen
to the negroes' breath.

Rifle barrels
are pointed at me,
I hear the smack
of the bullets.
Big Ben
has struck ten o'clock.

Revolving
out in space is
Vostok-6.

SIBYL OF CUMAE

In the church I had rather
speak five words
with my understanding...
Corinthians 14

Who calls
deep in sleep
affrighting me

Gale
heaving against
my neck
voices
voices
and between the eyebrows
suddenly
lightning

Then
shall I speak with tongues
in syllables
of stardust
and earth
in a language
that even
the
    empty
            space
which stands
between my words
shall still
speak

AT THIRTY-SIX

When I still drank water
from my cupped hand
under the damson tree,
at high noon.

Today
the world is
atomised,
electronic shadows
flit
through my hands.

Mathematics
has become our home,
atomic models
in the nurseries.

At nightfall
the birds take fright
at the sudden hush,
ears open,
and the poem,
not marked
on any map,
forgotten,
once more demands
to be heard.

FRANZ MARC

In a monastery garden
under the blue cloak
of the Virgin
the legend of his life,
the doe.

Later,
in the dry hoof-marks
from midnight
comes the wind,
the tower
of blue horses.

Towards nightfall,
under the Hartmannsweilerkopf
the trees show their rings,
the beasts show their veins,
the wolves sink their fangs
into the red
colour.

In the no-man's-land
under the skeletal trees
a night swallow,
dead,
with the moon's crescent
in its plumage.

MATHEMATICS

"And the angel of numbers
is flying
from 1 to 2..."
Rafael Alberti

The numbers
on our childhood slates
form ranks
when the angel with the integral
enters the room

He comes
with e^{-x}
with $\sqrt[\pi]{n}$
his tunic
is covered
with the snow of infinity

Angel of intuition
with your letters
we illumine
n-dimensional spaces
in the universe

Gone
the Euclidean tranquillity
of the world

STABAT MATER

Antonín Dvořák op.58

As a child
I carried your picture
in a porcelain medallion,
but the night
scattered ash into the prayer,
pathless the landscape leading to you,
snow is
covering it.

Mother of God,
intercessrix,
pray for us.

The Three Magi
no longer reach
the stable at Bethlehem,
experimental fields
on the cities' edges,
under gamma rays
the animals vegetate,
only the snake
survives.

Mother of God,
intercessrix,
I cannot feed
on heavenly bread alone,
in the midst of the cross,
where the beams intersect,
see, Mother,
your Son.

WARNING

Blinding bright clouds
in the taiga
the animals
flee to the north
the forest
stands
empty of birds

Hurricanes
break over the country
the flashes in the cloudbank
remain
fear like glue sticks
to our teeth

Fogbanks
are approaching
magnesium-green
the television screen
goes blank
rudderless
the ships drift
down the Danube

On our tongue
a blue
furry coating
the children
vomit their fathers' names
on the pavement

Disturbances
in the atmosphere
are increasing,
we can no longer
understand you
we hear
strange voices...

PASTORAL

An umbrella pine
in the rock,
olive trees
petrified
harder than stone,
the landing path
of the cranes
in the sedge.

In this landscape
the word
has not yet a false bottom,
here we live
between ochre and blue,
seperated
by a thin wall
of air.

Each morning,
when on the magnolia leaves
the mantis starts praying,
I get you
a handful of wind
from the treetops
for a dress,
and only at night
does memory splinter
among the twigs.

CLIO

I unrolled
your manuscripts
viewed parchments
under the magnifying glass
deciphered
signatures
and the seal
of kings

Under infra-red light
I traced
the palimpsests
but your scrolls
Clio
are frozen masks
skeletons

What am I to make
of the names of princes
of the date when the generals
took the field?

If you set off
on the voyage to Salamis
without seeing the oarsmen
in the hull of the ships
Clio remains
dead

MADRIGAL

I put a straw
as a ring
round your finger,
fragile and slim.

Landscape
with child's eyes,
in the mirror
of Bohemian ponds
we drew our names,
from star to star
I've drawn the lines,
a sky-chart
for your hand.

Along the bird routes,
where the letterboxes stand,
blue against blue,
the swallows carried
spring
into the land.

In November,
an ancient wayside cross,
the mountain wind smelled of snow,
from the mistletoe came the song
of a bird
of oblivion.

WOLFGANG AMADEUS MOZART

for Ewald Osers

In the front gardens,
where the rose-trees are,
on the window-sill
the blue jugs of milk,
the world
a sphere
of glass.

Constanze,
the greenness
climbing up the Leopoldsberg,
the vines cocooned
by autumn.

I have nothing
except a hat full of wind,
on the tree
where the mockingbird sits
the crows
are gathering.

Deep in snow
lies our time,
only at night,
across from the Salzach,
arrogant,
Don Giovanni's
scream.

ARNOLD SCHÖNBERG

A Survivor of Warsaw

Do you hear
how they link up,
the tone crystals
with the mother rock?

My notes:
grey zones,
twilight,
the melodies parched,
karstified.

Songs
caught
in the barbed wire.

Awaiting defilement
the Earth lies:
a
shroud.

WE, THE WORDS

I.

How often
have you betrayed the word
at the cock's
first crowing
You placed us
in Galvanic baths
hitched us
to the cart as your
Pegasus

You chased us
with dogs
you lined up
for our execution
in uniform
placed the syllables
in cruciform pattern
into the landscape

We the words
have gone grey
at the wailing wall
of speech

It may well be
that one day
you will not find us again
wordless
your body
reverts
to the beast

II.

At your deathbed
when all things
are like a cloudless sky
we shall arise before you
as mirror reflexions

We
are your last possession
all else in your houses
is
dust

MANUMITTED

Launching pads, academies,
where bacteria replace the sandtable,
what use the angel
with the flaming sword outside paradise?
Artificial suns
explode
over the skin of our earth,
a hail of quanta
drumming
on your body,
the stone begins to shriek,
outraged islands
plunge back into the ocean.

Nature
has manumitted you,
the forests are silent
and the rivers too
give you no answer:
you have come of age
you can crush your own image
in the ash,
or in the dust of the earth
plant roses.

IN THE WINE CELLAR

streaks of mist,
white,
chest-high.

Between the barrels
time wanders
soundlessly.

Don't tap the wood,
silence
encloses the wine
for years.

Between the syllables
silence
ripens.

WORDS

Flayed,
trampled
exiled,
brought back
and once more
denied.

I carry them
in my ear
as a cry,
as a lie
under my tongue,
they are the bread
of which I eat daily,
my body's invisible
clothes.

No games,
thickets of nettles.

And yet:
the most delicate structures,
dustless,
moulded by man.

OTHER VOLUMES OF POETRY TRANSLATED BY EWALD OSERS

Modern Czech Poetry (with J.K.Montgomery), Allen & Unwin, London 1945

Three Czech Poets (V.Nezval, A.Bartušek, J.Hanzlík), Penguin, London 1970

Selected Poems by Ondra Lysohorsky, Cape Editions, London 1971
Grossmann Publishers Inc., N.Y. 1971

Underseas Possessions : Selected Poems by Hans-Jürgen Heise,
Oleander Press, New York & Cambridge (England) 1972

With the Volume Turned Down & Other Poems by Reiner Kunze,
London Magazine Editions, London 1973

The Aztec Calendar & Other Poems by Antonín Bartušek,
Anvil Press, London 1975
Iowa Translation Series, Iowa 1975

Contemporary German Poetry, Oleander Press, N.Y. and Cambridge 1976

Strawberries in December & Other Poems by Hans Dieter Schäffer,
Carcanet Press, Cheadle 1976

Selected Poems by Rose Ausländer, London Magazine Editions 1977

Wounded No Doubt : Selected poems by Rudolf Langer,
Menard Press, London 1979

The Plague Column by Jaroslav Seifert, Terra Nova, London & Boston 1979

1001 Hayrens of Nahapet Kuckak, (13th Century Armenian love poetry,
Sovetakan grokh, Erevan 1979

Without Remission : Selected poems by Walter Helmut Fritz,
Menard Press, London 1981

An Umbrella from Piccadilly by Jaroslav Seifert, London Magazine Editions 1983

The Road to Freedom, Poems & Prose Poems by Geo Milev,
Sofia-Press, Sofia 1983

On the Contrary & Other Poems by Miroslav Holub,
Bloodaxe Books, Newcastle upon Tyne 1984

In Love With Life, an anthology of modern Czech poetry.
Artia Publishers, Prague 1984

Nineteen Poems by Nikola Vapsarov, Journeyman Press, London 1985

Selected Poems of Miroslav Válek, Tatran, Bratislavia (in preparation)

BIOGRAPHICAL AND BIBLIOGRAPHICAL NOTES

HANNS CIBULKA born 1920 in Jägerndorf, in the German-speaking border region of Czechoslovakia. Prisoner-of-war until 1948. Now a librarian in Gotha, German Democratic Republic.

Märzlicht (poems) 1959

Sizilianisches Tagebuch (prose) 1960

Arioso (poems) 1962

Umbrische Tage (prose) 1963

Windrose (poems) 1968

Sanddornzeit (prose) 1971

Dornburger Blätter (prose) 1972

Lichtschwalben (poems) 1973

Liebeserklärung in K (prose) 1974

Tagebücher (collected prose) 1976

Der Lebensbaum (poems) 1977

Der Rebstock (poems) 1980

The poems in this volume are from *Windrose, Lebensbaum, Lichtschwalben* and *Der Rebstock*. (All published by Mitteldeutschee Verlag, Halle/Saale, German Democratic Republic)